COLLECTED POEMS

also by Stephen Spender

poetry
SELECTED POEMS
THE OEDIPUS TRILOGY
A CHOICE OF SHELLEY'S VERSE

autobiography
WORLD WITHIN WORLD

JOURNALS 1939–1983
edited by John Goldsmith

STEPHEN SPENDER

*Collected Poems
1928-1985*

faber and faber

LONDON · BOSTON

First published in 1985
by Faber and Faber Limited
3 Queen Square London WC1N 3AU

Photoset by Wilmaset Birkenhead Wirral
Printed in Great Britain by
Redwood Burn Ltd
Trowbridge Wiltshire
All rights reserved

British Library Cataloguing in Publication Data

Spender, Stephen
Collected poems.
I. Title
821'.912   PR6037.P47

ISBN 0–571–13698–2
ISBN 0–571–13666–4 Pbk

Contents

IX HOME

X LANDSCAPE AND SEASCAPE

XI DIARY POEMS

Introduction

A volume of *Collected Poems* contains those poems by which a poet would wish to be remembered. In putting together this volume I find that my judgement of my own poetry has changed considerably since I published a collection in 1955. This is partly because there are, inevitably, more poems to choose from, but partly also because I now think that my best poems are those which are extremely clear and that, perhaps without my being fully aware of it, clarity has always been my aim. At any rate, the poems I have thrown out are those which seem to me confused or verbose. Those that I have put in, for the most part are simple and straightforward. This also means that I have included here some early poems that I did not put in that first volume, notably versions – one poem each – of Rilke, Lorca and Altolaguirre.

In re-working poems I have always done so with the sense that in writing a poem I have certain intentions which I very rarely forget. If I take up a notebook and find in it a sketch for a poem which I made many years ago, I can remember exactly what I was setting out to do, and I sometimes find that I can continue it as though I had written the sketch yesterday. In re-writing some poems here I have always gone back to first intentions and to memory of the circumstances from which the poem arose.

Over the years, there are many friends to whom I am grateful for criticism and suggestion, but I would particularly like to thank Peter Ackroyd for going through poems I showed him recently and for suggesting improvements.

26 February 1985

I PRELUDES

Airman

He will watch the hawk with an indifferent eye
    Or pitifully;
Nor on those eagles that so feared him, now
    Will strain his brow;
Weapons men use, stone, sling and strong-thewed bow
    He will not know.

This aristocrat, superb of all instinct.
    With death close-linked
Had paced the enormous cloud, almost had won
    War on the sun;
Till now, like Icarus mid-ocean-drowned,
    Hands, wings, are found.

Autumn Day

after Rilke

Lord, it is time. The summer was so great.
Lay down long shadows on the sundials.
Let loose the winds to run across the plain.

Command the lingering fruits to ripen:
Grant them two southerly days yet
Then drive them to fulfilment and compel
The final sweetness in the heavy wine.

Who has no house, will build himself none now;
Who is alone now, will stay so –
Wake, read, write long letters, go
Back and forth along bare avenues,
Restlessly wandering, where the fallen leaves blow.

Cornet Cornelius Rilke

Rolled over on Europe: the sharp dew frozen to stars
Below us; above our heads, the night
Frozen again to stars; the stars
In pools between our coats; and that charmed moon.
Ah, what supports? What cross draws out our arms,
Heaves up our bodies towards the wind
And hammers us between the mirrored lights?

Only my body is real: which wolves
Are free to oppress and gnaw. Only this rose
My friend laid on my breast, and these few lines
Written from home, are real.

Beethoven's Death Mask

I imagine him still with heavy brow.
Huge, black, with bent head and falling hair,
He ploughs the landscape. His face
Is this hanging mask transfigured,
This mask of death which the white lights make stare.

I see the thick hands clasped; the scarecrow coat;
The light strike upwards at the holes for eyes;
The beast squat in that mouth whose opening is
The hollow opening of an organ pipe:
There the wind sings and the harsh longing cries.

He moves across my vision like a ship.
What else is iron but he? The fields divide
And, heaving, are changing waters of the sea.
He is prisoned, masked, shut off from Being.
Life, like a fountain, he sees leap – outside.

Yet, in that head, there twists the roaring cloud
And coils, as in a shell, the roaring wave.
The damp leaves whisper; bending to the rain
The April rises in him, chokes his lungs
And climbs the torturing passage of his brain.

Then the drums move away, the Distance shows:
Now cloud-hid peaks are bared; the mystic One
Horizons haze, as the blue incense, heaven.
Peace . . . peace . . . Then splitting skull and dream,
                                    there comes
Blotting our lights, the Trumpeter, the sun.

Never Being

Never being, but always on the edge of Being,
My head – Death Mask – is brought into the sun.
With shadow pointing finger across cheek,
I move lips for tasting, I move hands for touching,
But never come nearer than touching
Though Spirit lean outward for seeing.
Observing rose, gold, eyes, an admired landscape,
My senses record the act of wishing,
Wishing to be,
Rose, gold, landscape or another.
I claim fulfilment on the fact of loving.

Trigorin

An 'I' can never be great man.
This known great one has weakness
To friends is most remarkable for weakness:
His ill-temper at meals, dislike of being contradicted,
His only real pleasure, fishing in ponds,
His only real wish – forgetting.

To advance from friends to the composite self,
Central 'I' is surrounded by 'I eating'
'I loving', 'I angry', 'I excreting',
But the great 'I' planted in him
Has nothing to do with all these

Can never claim its true place
Resting in the forehead, secure in his gaze.
The great 'I' is an unfortunate intruder
Quarrelling with 'I tiring' and 'I sleeping'
And all those other 'I's, who long for 'We dying'.

My Parents

My parents kept me from children who were rough
Who threw words like stones and wore torn clothes
Their thighs showed through rags they ran in the street
And climbed cliffs and stripped by the country streams.

I feared more than tigers their muscles like iron
Their jerking hands and their knees tight on my arms
I feared the salt coarse pointing of those boys
Who copied my lisp behind me on the road.

They were lithe they sprang out behind hedges
Like dogs to bark at my world. They threw mud
While I looked the other way, pretending to smile.
I longed to forgive them but they never smiled.

What I Expected

What I expected, was
Thunder, fighting,
Long struggles with men
And climbing.
After continual straining
I should grow strong;
Then the rocks would shake
And I rest long.

What I had not foreseen
Was the gradual day
Weakening the will
Leaking the brightness away,
The lack of good to touch,
The fading of body and soul
Smoke before wind,
Corrupt, unsubstantial.

The wearing of Time,
And the watching of cripples pass
With limbs shaped like questions
In their odd twist,
The pulverous grief
Melting the bones with pity,
The sick falling from earth –
These, I could not foresee.

Expecting always
Some brightness to hold in trust
Some final innocence
Exempt from dust,
That, hanging solid,
Would dangle through all
Like the created poem,
Or the faceted crystal.

Marston

Marston, dropping it in the grate, broke his pipe.
Nothing hung on this act, it was no symbol
Prophetic for calamity, but merely ludicrous.

That heavy-wrought briar with the great pine face
Now split across like a boxer's hanging dream
Of punishing a nigger, he brought from the continent:
It was his absurd relic, like bones,
Of stamping on the white-face mountains,
Early beds in huts, and other journeys.

To hold the banks of the Danube, the slow barges down
                                        the river,
Those coracles with faces painted on,
Demanded his last money,
A foodless journey home, as pilgrimage.

Not to you

Not to you I sighed. No, not a word.
We climbed together. Any feeling was
Formed with the hills. It was like trees' unheard
And monumental sign of country peace.

But next day, stumbling, panting up dark stairs,
Rushing in room and door flung wide, I knew.
Oh empty walls, book-carcases, blank chairs
All splintered in my head and cried for you.

Acts passed beyond

Acts passed beyond the boundary of mere wishing
Not privy looks, hedged words, at times you saw.
These blundering, heart-surrendered troopers were
Small presents made, and waiting for the tram.
Then once you said: 'Waiting was very kind',
And looked surprised. Surprising for me, too,
Whose every movement had been missionary,
A pleading tongue unheard. I had not thought
That you, who nothing else saw, would see this.

So 'very kind' was merest overflow
Something I had not reckoned in myself,
A chance deserter from my force. When we touched hands,
I felt the whole rebel, feared mutiny
And turned away,
Thinking, if these were tricklings through a dam,
I must have love enough to run a factory on,
Or give a city power, or drive a train.

The Photograph

How it reminds me of that day!
Walking alone without you,
Remembering your voice
And looking at your face, to take this photograph:
The river curving behind branches,
Mist expunging the dark water,
Fragments of sun like shattered mirrors
Scattered through ditches, and you leaning over
The map of everywhere we'd been.

The Truly Great

I think continually of those who were truly great.
Who, from the womb, remembered the soul's history
Through corridors of light, where the hours are suns,
Endless and singing. Whose lovely ambition
Was that their lips, still touched with fire,
Should tell of the Spirit, clothed from head to foot in song.
And who hoarded from the Spring branches
The desires falling across their bodies like blossoms.

What is precious, is never to forget
The essential delight of the blood drawn from ageless springs
Breaking through rocks in worlds before our earth.
Never to deny its pleasure in the morning simple light
Nor its grave evening demand for love.
Never to allow gradually the traffic to smother
With noise and fog, the flowering of the spirit.

Near the snow, near the sun, in the highest fields,
See how these names are fêted by the waving grass
And by the streamers of white cloud
And whispers of wind in the listening sky.
The names of those who in their lives fought for life,
Who wore at their hearts the fire's centre.
Born of the sun, they travelled a short while toward the sun
And left the vivid air signed with their honour.

The Sign *Faehre nach Wilm*

At the end of our Ruegen holiday, that night,
I lay awake. Waves' ceaseless fretful scansion
By imagination scourged, rose to the height
Of the town's roar, trafficking apprehension.
I was in a train . . . On a film's played back spool
I watched speeding reversed the things that heal
Angst. The sign *'Faehre nach Wilm'*.
The pink cottage by the lake, shone brilliant, yet unreal.
Real were iron lines, track smashing the grass,
Wheels on which we rode, and, on our wrists, time.
Unreal were cattle, wave-winged storks, the lime.
These glowed in a lost planet seen through glass,
Like 'Rose' or 'Friend' in a forgotten rhyme.

Us

Oh young men oh young comrades
it is too late now to stay in those houses
your fathers built where they built you to breed
money on money it is too late
to make or to count what was made

Count rather those fabulous possessions
which begin with your body and your burning soul
the hairs on your skin the muscles extending
in ranges with lakes across your limbs

Count your eyes as jewels and your golden sex
then count the sun and innumerable lights
sparkling on waves and spangled on the soil
　　It is too late now to stay in those houses where
　　　　　　　　　　　　　　　　　　　the ghosts are
ladies like flies imprisoned in amber
financiers like fossils of fish in coal.

Oh comrades step forth from the solid stone
advance to rebuilt and sleep with friend on hill
advance to rebel and remember what you have

ghost never had entombed in his hall.

Helmut

Alas, when he laughs, it is not he
But a shopkeeper, who scrapes his hands, and bows,
Seller of ties and shirts who shows his teeth
Even out of hours. If he could laugh that laugh
Matching his glinting naked hair
And the jungle crouched beneath his eyelashes
I think the barrier
That shuts out all his sky and grows
Between us and the dark pools of his will,
Would fall; the rocks
Burst with German streams again.

Shadow of War

Who live under the shadow of a war,
What can I do that matters?
My pen stops, and my laughter, dancing, stop
Or ride to a gap.

How often, on the powerful crest of pride,
I am shot with thought
That halts the untamed horses of the blood,
The grip on good:

That moving, whimpering and mating bear
Tunes to deaf ears:
Stuffed with the realer passions of the earth
Beneath this hearth.

In 1929

I

A whim of Time, the general arbiter,
Proclaims the love, instead of death, of friends.
Under the domed sky and athletic sun
Three stand naked: the new, bronzed German
The communist clerk, and myself, being English.

Yet to unwind the travelled sphere twelve years
Then two take arms, spring to a soldier's posture:
Or else roll on the thing a further ten,
The third – this clerk with world-offended eyes –
Builds with red hands his heaven: makes our bones
The necessary scaffolding to peace.

II

Now, I suppose, the once-envious dead
Have learned a strict philosophy of clay
After long centuries, to haunt us no longer
In the churchyard or at the end of the lane
Or howling at the edge of the city
Beyond the last bean rows, near the new factory.

Our fathers killed. And yet there lives no feud
Like Hamlet's, prompted on the castle stair:
There falls no shadow on our blank of peace,
We three together, struck across our path,
No warning finger threatening each alone.

III

Our fathers' misery, their spirits' mystery,
The cynic's cruelty, weave this philosophy:
That the history of man, traced purely from dust,
Is lipping skulls on the revolving rim
Or war, us three each other's murderers –

Lives, risen a moment, joined or separate,
Fall heavily, then are ever separate,
Sod lifted, turned, slapped back again with spade.

Hamburg, 1929

Hopelessly wound round with the cords of streets
Men travel down their lines of level graves.
Sometimes the maze knots into flaring caves
Where magic-lantern faces tilt their greetings.
Smiles dawn with a harsh lightning, there's no speaking,
And, far from lapping laughter, all's cramped and hard.
Here the pale lily boys flaunt their bright lips,
Such guilty cups for money, and older whores
Scuttle rat-toothed into the night outdoors.

Northwards, the sea exerts his huge mandate.
His guardians, furnace beams, like candles stand,
Flashing Pharos, and hammering from yards.
In their lush gardens, merchants dwell, southwards
Well-fed, well-lit, well-spoken men are these,
With bronze-faced sons and happy in their daughters.

Van der Lubbe

O staring eyes, searchlight disks,
Listen at my lips. I am louder than to
Swim prize-winning Channel or to grapple
Up this town's tallest steeple.

I throw you my words, whatever comes first,
You must eat my scraps and dance.
I am glad I am glad that this people is mad
To drink in my newsreel dance.

Why do you laugh? My black-robed judge asks.
I laugh at this trial although it will make
My life end at a gate.
Axe severing a stalk.

Yes. No. Yes. No. Shall I tell you what I know?
Not to Goering, but, dear microphone, to you.
I laugh because my laughter
Is like German justice, twisted by a howitzer.

The senses are shaken from the judging heart,
The eye turned inwards, and the outside world
Into the grave of the skull rolled
With no stars riding heaven, and disparate.

The twisting of justice, the stuttering of guns
Splintering trees where once on their branches
Truth greenly balanced, are what I am –
Whom you sentence to death and spits at you in fun.

The Pylons

The secret of these hills was stone, and cottages
Of that stone made,
And crumbling roads
That turned on sudden hidden villages.

Now over these small hills, they have built the concrete
That trails black wire;
Pylons, those pillars
Bare like nude, giant girls that have no secret.

The valley with its gilt and evening look
And the green chestnut
Of customary root,
Are mocked dry like the parched bed of a brook.

But far above and far as sight endures
Like whips of anger
With lightning's danger
There runs the quick perspective of the future.

This dwarfs our emerald country by its trek
So tall with prophecy:
Dreaming of cities
Where often clouds shall lean their swan-white neck.

The Express

After the first powerful plain manifesto
The black statement of pistons, without more fuss
But gliding like a queen, she leaves the station.
Without bowing and with restrained unconcern
She passes the houses which humbly crowd outside,
The gasworks, and at last the heavy page
Of death, printed by gravestones in the cemetery.
Beyond the town, there lies the open country
Where, gathering speed, she acquires mystery,
The luminous self-possession of ships on ocean.
It is now she begins to sing – at first quite low
Then loud, and at last with a jazzy madness –
The song of her whistle screaming at curves,
Of deafening tunnels, brakes, innumerable bolts.
And always light, aerial underneath
Retreats the elate metre of her wheels.
Steaming through metal landscape on her lines,
She plunges new eras of white happiness
Where speed throws up strange shapes, broad curves
And parallels clean like trajectories from guns.
At last, further than Edinburgh or Rome,
Beyond the crest of the world, she reaches night
Where only a low stream-line brightness
Of phosphorus, on the tossing hills is white.
Ah, like a comet through flame, she moves entranced
Wrapt in her music no bird-song, no, nor bough,
Breaking with honey buds, shall ever equal.

The Landscape Near an Aerodrome

More beautiful and soft than any moth
With burring furred antennae feeling its huge path
Through dusk, the air liner with shut-back engines
Glides over suburbs and the sleeves set trailing tall
To point the wind. Gently, broadly, she falls
Scarcely disturbing charted currents of air.

Lulled by descent, the travellers across sea
And across feminine land indulging its easy limbs
In miles of softness, now let their eyes trained by watching
Penetrate through dusk the outskirts of this town
Here where industry shows a fraying edge.
Here they can see what is being done.

Beyond the winking masthead light
And the landing ground, they observe the outposts
Of work: chimneys like lank black fingers
Or figures, frightening and mad: and squat buildings
With their strange air behind trees, like women's faces
Shattered by grief. Here where few houses
Moan with faint light behind their blinds
They remark the unhomely sense of complaint, like a dog
Shut out, and shivering at the foreign moon.

In the last sweep of love, they pass over fields
Behind the aerodrome, where boys play all day
Hacking dead grass: whose cries, like wild birds,
Settle upon the nearest roofs
But soon are hid under the loud city.

Then, as they land, they hear the tolling bell
Reaching across the landscape of hysteria,
To where, louder than all those batteries,
And charcoaled towers against that dying sky,
Religion stands, the church blocking the sun.

Perhaps

The explosion of a bomb –
The submarine – a bubble pricked by water –
Dollfuss clutching his shot arm –
The Reichstag that the Nazis set on fire –
And then our Party forbidden –

Motorcycles wires aeroplanes cars trains
Converging on that town Geneva –
Top hats plotting at the lake's edge
And the Alps beyond –

Headlines pour from rotating cylinders
Sheets from paper rolls.
Newsboys spread in compass points across
Maps, the four directions of the winds.

Was that final when they shot him? Did that war
Lop off dead branches? Are we the bright new shoots?
Is it Leviathan, that revolution
Nosing through icebergs of the Arctic wastes?

Only Perhaps. It may be we are withered
Those headlines only walls around our coffin
Dry dice rattled in a bony box

Can be illusion of things merely changing

Perhaps some Unknown God is newly risen
Beyond the lake, or crucified

Perhaps our time is

Monstrous with stillness like that Alpine range.

Unemployed

Moving through the silent crowd
Who stand behind dull cigarettes,
These men who idle in the road,
I have the sense of falling light.

They lounge at corners of the street
And greet friends with a shrug of shoulder
And turn their empty pockets out,
The cynical gestures of the poor.

Now they've no work, like better men
Who sit at desks and take much pay
They sleep long nights and rise at ten
To watch the hours that drain away.

I'm jealous of the weeping hours
They stare through with such hungry eyes
I'm haunted by these images,
I'm haunted by their emptiness.

An Elementary School Classroom in a Slum

Far far from gusty waves these children's faces.
Like rootless weeds, the hair torn round their pallor:
The tall girl with her weighed-down head. The paper-
seeming boy, with rat's eyes. The stunted, unlucky heir
Of twisted bones, reciting a father's gnarled disease,
His lesson, from his desk. At back of the dim class
One unnoted, sweet and young. His eyes live in a dream
Of squirrel's game, in tree room, other than this.

On sour cream walls, donations. Shakespeare's head,
Cloudless at dawn, civilized dome riding all cities.
Belled, flowery, Tyrolese valley. Open-handed map
Awarding the world its world. And yet, for these
Children, these windows, not this map, their world,
Where all their future's painted with a fog,
A narrow street sealed in with a lead sky
Far far from rivers, capes, and stars of words.

Surely, Shakespeare is wicked, the map a bad example,
With ships and sun and love tempting them to steal –
For lives that slyly turn in their cramped holes
From fog to endless night? On their slag heap, these children
Wear skins peeped through by bones and spectacles of steel
With mended glass, like bottle bits on stones.
All of their time and space are foggy slum.
So blot their maps with slums as big as doom.

Unless, governor, inspector, visitor,
This map becomes their window and these windows
That shut upon their lives like catacombs,
Break O break open till they break the town
And show the children to green fields, and make their world
Run azure on gold sands, and let their tongues
Run naked into books the white and green leaves open
History theirs whose language is the sun.

The Prisoners

Far far the least of all, in want,
Are these,
The prisoners
Turned massive with their vaults and dark with dark.

They raise no hands, which rest upon their knees,
But lean their solid eyes against the night
Dimly they feel
Only the furniture they use in cells.

Their Time is almost Death. The silted flow
Of years on years
Is marked by dawns
As faint as cracks on mud-flats of despair.

My pity moves amongst them like a breeze
On walls of stone,
Fretting for summer leaves, or like a tune
On ears of stone.

Then, when I raise my hands to strike,
It is too late,
There are no chains that fall,
Nor visionary liquid door
Melted with anger.

When have their lives been free from walls and dark
And airs that choke?
Where less prisoner, to let my anger
Like a sun strike?

[48]

If I could follow them from room to womb
To plant some hope
Through the black silk of the big-bellied gown,
There would I win.

Alas,
It is too late for anger,
Nothing prevails
But pity for the grief they cannot feel.

Not Palaces

Not palaces, an era's crown
Where the mind dwells, intrigues, rests:
Architectural gold-leaved flower
From people ordered like a single mind,
I build: this only what I tell:
It is too late for rare accumulation,
For family pride, for beauty's filtered dusts;
I say, stamping the words with emphasis,
Drink from here energy and only energy
To will this time's change.
Eye, gazelle, delicate wanderer,
Drinker of horizon's fluid line;
Ear that suspends on a chord
The spirit drinking timelessness;
Touch, love, all senses;
Leave your gardens, your singing feasts,
Your dreams of suns circling before our sun,
Of heaven after our world.
Instead, watch images of flashing glass
That strike the outward sense, the polished will,
Flag of our purpose which the wind engraves.
No spirit seek here rest. But this: No one
Shall hunger: Man shall spend equally;
Our goal which we compel: Man shall be man.

In Railway Halls

In railway halls, on pavements near the traffic,
They beg, their eyes made big by empty staring
And only measuring Time, like the blank clock.

No, I shall weave no tracery of pen ornament
To make them birds upon my singing tree:
Time merely drives these lives which do not live
As tides push rotten stuff along the shore.

– There is no consolation, no, none,
In the curving beauty of that line
Traced on our graphs through History, where the oppressor
Starves and deprives the poor.

Paint here no draped despairs, no saddening clouds
Where the soul rests, proclaims eternity.
But let the wrong cry out as raw as wounds
This time forgets and never heals, far less transcends.

II   EXILES

Polar Exploration

Pour n'être pas changés en bêtes, ils s'enivrent
D'espace et de lumière et de cieux embrasés;
La glace qui les mord, les soleils qui les cuivrent,
Effacent lentement la marque des baisers.

Baudelaire

Our single purpose was to walk through snow:
As clerks in whited banks with bird-claw pens
Leave tracks columned on paper,
To snow we added footprints.
Soon total whiteness drowned
All sense of space. We trudged through
Static, glaring days, time's suspended blank.
That was in spring, and autumn. Summer struck
Water over rocks, and half our world
Became a ship with a deep keel near booming floes
And icebergs run across by little birds –
Twittering Snow Bunting, Greenland Wheatear,
Red-throated Divers. Imagine butterflies
Sulphurous clouded yellow: burnish of bees
That suck from saxifrage.
There followed winter in a frozen hut
Warm enough at the kernel, but should you sleep
With head against the wall – ice glued my hair.
Hate Culver's loud breathing, despise Freeman's
Fidget for washing; love only the dogs
That whine for scraps, and scratch. Notice
How they run better (on short journeys) with a bitch –
In that, different from us.

Return, return, you warn. I do. There is
Your city – railways, money, words, words, words,
Banks, banquets, newspapers, debates
Cinema, radio. The worst is Marriage.
I cannot sleep. At night, I hear
A voice speak through white rifts. Was
Ice, your anger transformed? The raw, the motionless
Skies, were these the spirit's hunger?
The unending hypnotic march through snow
The dropping nights of precious extinction, were these
Only the will's evasion? Is the North,
Over there, a palpable real madness
A glittering folly, one without towns,
Only with birds and bears and fish, a cyclops eye,
A new and singular sex?

The Uncreating Chaos
(Double Portrait in a Mirror)

I

To the meeting despair of eyes in the street, offer
Your eyes on plates and your liver on skewers of pity.
When the Jericho sky is heaped with clouds which the sun
Trumpets above, respond to Apocalypse
With a headache. In spirit follow
The young men to the war, up Everest. Be shot.

For the uncreating chaos
Claims you in marriage: though a man, you were ever
                                        a bride.
Ever among the supple surface of summer-brown muscle
The fountaining evening chatter under the stars,
The student who chucks back his forelock in front of a glass,
You only longed for your longing to last.

The engine in you, anxiety,
Is a grave lecher, a globe-trotter, one
With moods of straw, the winds that blow him, aeroplanes.
'Whatever happens, I shall never be alone,
I shall always have a fare, an affair, or a revolution.'

II

I am so close to you
I will confess to you
I am all that you do.

In thoughts where pity is the same as cruelty
Your life is mine. Whether
What fears and falters is myself
Or yourself – all
The apprehension of this time,
We are both one.

At night I'm flooded by the future
Incoming tide of the unharnessed war.

Beyond the blacked-out windows of our nightmare
Facts race their hundred miles an hour
In iron circles on an iron plain.
The riders of those race-cars lose
All sense of where they are.
Ridden by their speed, the men
Are their machines.

III

All I can foresee now – more I shall learn –
Is that our fear creates its opposite.
Our peace is war.
When you choose a mirror for a lover
It shows you your own image as a gunman.
You are a ghost amid the flares of shellfire
Less living than
The last war dead whose veins of mineral
We mine for here.

IV

Shall I ever reach
The field enclosed by stones
In the high mountains
Where the scytheless wind
Flushes the swayed grasses?
Where clouds without rain
Add to the sun
Their mirroring shine?
The simple machinery is here
Clear room clear day clear desk
And the hand with its power
To make the heart pour
Into the word, as the sun
Moves upward through the corn.
Meanwhile, where nothing's sacred
And love no longer willed
Nor our true purpose conscious,
Holy is lucidity
And the mind that dare explain.

Solipsist

He is one of
The human machines
So common on the khaki plains.
Here and Now made flesh
Senses
Crammed with all the world outside.

And if he were to die
The world would fly
In Judgement Day
To the ends of the sky
Colour of the colour of his eye.

Waking each morning, he thinks
'Let there be light.' There is
Because he is,

Sleeping each night, he goes
Into a sightless coffin
Where all the world outside
– Earth air water fire
All that most devours –
Proves it exists.

A Footnote

from Marx's chapter in *Das Capital*,
'The Working Day'

'Heard say that four times four is eight,'
'And the king is the man what has all the Gold'
'And our King is a Queen and her son's a Princess
'And they live in a Palace called London, I'm told.'

'Heard say that a man who's called God who's a Dog
'Made the World, with us in it.' 'And then I've heard
'There came a great Flood and the World was all Drowned,
'Except for one Man and that Man was a Bird.'

'Perhaps all the People are dead and we're Birds
'Shut in steel cages by Satan, who's Good,
'And the Miners in their Pit Cages
'And us in our Chimneys to climb, as we should.'

– Ah twittering voices
Of children crawling on their knees
At foot of the most crowded pages
Of Blue Books, histories,
You are the birds of a songless age
Young like the youngest gods, awarded
Mythical childhood always.
Often I see clouds
In sunsets above London
Drawn back like a curtain
To show a sky in which there float
Putti and cherubim
Of an insensate ignorant age.

[61]

The Exiles

History has tongues
Has angels has guns
    Has saved has praised
Her exiles-in-life death-returned
      For whom her printed page
Is heaven on which their names write worlds.

III SPAIN

Adam

after García Lorca

Morning by tree of blood is moistened
Where the newly delivered woman groans.
Her voice leaves crystals in the wound
And in the window a print of bones.

While the light comes in secure and gains
White boundaries of oblivious fable
In the race from the turmoil of the veins
Into the clouded coolness of the apple,

Adam dreams in the fever of clay
Of a child who draws near galloping
With the double throb of his cheek its way.

But another darker Adam sleeping
Dreams of neuter seedless stone moon afar
Where the child of light is kindling.

Port Bou

As a child holds a pet
Arms clutching but with hands that do not join
And the coiled animal looks through the gap
To outer freedom, of animal air,
So the earth and rock arms of this harbour
Embrace but do not encircle the sea,
Which, through a gap, vibrates into that freedom
Where dolphins swim and liners throb.
In the bright winter sunlight I sit on the parapet
Of a bridge; my circling arms rest on a newspaper
And my mind is empty as the glittering stone
While I search for an image
To set down the toy-like headlands of Port Bou.
With creaking brakes a lorry halts beside me
And I look up at crinkling flag-like faces
Of militia men staring at my newspaper from France.
'How do they write of our struggle over the frontier?'
I hold out the newspaper but they cannot read,
They want talk and to offer cigarettes.
In their smiles the war finds peace. The famished mouths
Of rusted carbines lean against their knees
And wrapped in cloth – old granny in a shawl –
The stammering machine-gun rests.
They shout – wave – as the truck jerks forward
Over the tufty hill, and beyond the headland.
An old man passes, his mouth dribbling,
Through rusted teeth he spits out 'pom! pom! pom!'
The children follow, and, more slowly, women
Clutching their skirts, go over the horizon.

Now Port Bou is emptied, for the firing practice.
I am left alone on the parapet at the exact centre
Above the river trickling through the gulley, like that
                                             old man's spittle.
I am alone like the bull's eye on a target.
Nothing moves against my background of houses like
                                             its cardboard
Save disgraceful skirring dogs. The firing now begins
Across the harbour mouth, headland to headland,
White flecks of foam whipped by lead on the water
An echo like a cat-o'nine-tails
Lashing the flanks of the surrounding hills.
My clenching arms rest on the newspaper
My mind seems paper on which thoughts blow dust,
I assure myself the shooting is for practice
But fear is all I feel. The machine gun stitches
My intestines with a needle, back and forth:
The solitary spasmodic white puffs from the carbine
Draw fear in white threads back and forth through my body.

The Room above the Square

The light in the window seemed perpetual
When you stayed in the high room for me;
It glowed above the trees through leaves
Like my certainty.

The light is fallen and you are hidden
In sunbright peninsulas of the sword:
Torn like leaves through Europe is the peace
That through us flowed.

Now I climb alone to the high room
Above the darkened square
Where among stones and roots, the other
Unshattered lovers are.

Ultima Ratio Regum

The guns spell money's ultimate reason
In letters of lead on the Spring hillside.
But the boy lying dead under the olive trees
Was too young and too silly
To have been notable to their important eye.
He was a better target for a kiss.

When he lived, tall factory hooters never summoned him
Nor did restaurant plate glass windows revolve to wave
him in
His name never appeared in the papers.
The world maintained its traditional wall
Round the dead with their gold sunk deep as a well
Whilst his life, intangible as a Stock Exchange rumour,
drifted outside.

O too lightly he threw down his cap
One day when the breeze threw petals from the trees.
The unflowering wall sprouted with guns
Machine gun anger quickly scythed the grasses;
Flags and leaves fell from hands and branches;
The tweed cap rotted in the nettles.

Consider his life which was valueless
In terms of employment, hotel ledgers, news files.
Consider. One bullet in ten thousand kills a man.
Ask. Was so much expenditure justified
On the death of one so young, and so silly,
Lying under the olive trees, O world, O death?

The Coward

Under the olive trees, from the ground
Grows this flower, which is a wound.
It is wiser to ignore
Than the hero's medalled hour.
Blazing with flags on the world's shore.
Its blood-black petals have no name
Except the coward's hidden shame.
Here one died, not like a soldier,
From gun-shot, but the void of terror.
His final moment was the birth
Of the revelatory truth:
That the transport at the quay,
His mother's care, his lover's kiss,
The waving handkerchiefs of spray,
All led him to this emptiness:
All the fantasies betrayed,
Flesh, bones, muscles, eyes,
Assembled in a tower of lies,
Scattered on the icy breeze,
Dreams of victory in one instant
Changed to this unchanging present,
Death under the olive trees.

To populate his loneliness
And to bring his ghost release
Love and pity dare not cease
For a lifetime, at the least.

A Stopwatch and an Ordnance Map

To Samuel Barber

A stopwatch and an ordnance map.
At five a man fell to the ground.
And the watch flew from his wrist
Like a moon struck from the earth
Marking a blank time that stares
On the tides of change beneath.
All under the olive trees.

A stopwatch and an ordnance map.
He stayed faithfully in that place
From his living comrade split
By dividers of the bullet
Opening wide the distances
Of his final loneliness.
All under the olive trees.

A stopwatch and an ordnance map.
And the bones are fixed at five
Under the moon's timelessness.
But another who lives on
Wears within his heart for ever
Space split open by the bullet.
All under the olive trees.

Two Armies

Deep as the winter plain, two armies
Dig their machinery, to destroy each other.
Men freeze and hunger. No one is given leave
On either side, except the dead, and wounded.
These have their leave; while new battalions wait
On time at last to bring them violent peace.

All have become so nervous and so cold
That each man hates the cause and distant words
That brought him here, more terribly than bullets.
Once a boy hummed a popular marching song.
Once a novice hand flapped their salute;
The voice was choked, the upraised fist fell
Shot through the wrist by those of his own side.

From their numb harvest all would flee, except
For discipline drilled in an iron school
Which holds them at the point of the revolver.
Yet when they sleep, the images of home
Ride wishing horses of escape
Which herd the plain in a mass unspoken poem.

Finally, they cease to hate: for although hate
Bursts from the air and whips the earth with hail
Or shoots it up in fountains to marvel at,
And although hundreds fall, who can connect
The inexhaustible anger of the guns
With the dumb patience of these animals?

Clean silence drops at night, when a little walk
Divides the sleeping armies, each
Huddled in linen woven by remote hands.
When the machines are stilled, a common suffering
Whitens the air with breath and makes both one
As though these enemies slept in each other's arms.

Only the lucid friend to aerial raiders
The brilliant pilot moon, stares down
Upon this plain she makes a shining bone
Cut by the shadows of many thousand bones.
Where amber clouds scatter on No-Man's-Land
She regards Death and Time throw up
The furious words and minerals that destroy.

Thoughts During an Air Raid

Of course, the entire effort is to put oneself
Outside the ordinary range
Of what are called statistics. A hundred are killed
In the outer suburbs. Well, well, *one* carries on.
So long as this thing 'I' is propped up on
The girdered bed which seems so like a hearse,
In the hotel bedroom with the wallpaper
Blowing smoke wreaths of roses, *one* can ignore
The pressure of those names under the fingers
Indented by lead type on newsprint,
In the bar, the marginal wailing wireless.
Yet, supposing that a bomb should dive
Its nose right through this bed, with *one* upon it?
The thought's obscene. Still, there are many
For whom one's loss would demonstrate
The 'impersonal' use indeed. The essential is
That every *one* should remain separate
Propped up under roses, and no one suffer
For his neighbour. Then horror is postponed
Piecemeal for each, until it settles on him
That wreath of incommunicable grief
Which is all mystery or nothing.

My Brother Luis

after Manuel Altolaguirre

My brother Luis
Used to kiss me, shyly,
On railway platforms.
He always waited for me
Or went with me to say goodbye
And now
He's left me, going away I don't know where,
I was not there in time,
I found no one.
Not even the most distant echo
Not a shadow
Nor my own reflection on white clouds.
This sky is too immense.
Where are my brother's sons?
Why are they not here?
I'd like to walk with them
Among real things.
Perhaps they would give me his photograph.
I don't want them to be in a room
Wearing black clothes.
It would be better if they ran by the river,
If they ran among flowers without looking at them,
Themselves like flowers,
Like boys
Who never stop
As I have stopped
Too close to the edge of the sea and of death.

To Manuel Altolaguirre

You stared out of the window at the emptiness
Of a world exploding
– Walls hurled upwards in a fountain
Dust blown sideways by the wind.
Every sensation left you
But that of being alone
With no fixed object for the eye to fix on.
You were a child again
Seeing for the first time how things happen.

Stupidly then the stucco pigeon
Stuck on the gable above your ceiling
Pirouetted outside your window
Uttering, as it did so, a loud coo.
Then everything in the room broke
Only you stayed whole
Wondering if you'd turned into your soul,
And no one with you there to share the joke.

The blood! The blood! It streamed down from your forehead.
Your fingers felt to see if you were dead.
You weren't. Proud of your wound you went
To show it like a medal to your neighbours.

'But when I got to the next floor,
'Through their wide open door,
'Beyond the banisters,
'I saw them all spread out on chairs.
' – Grandparents, father, mother, children.
'All twelve in bandages,
'And two in splints, and one on crutches . . .

'What could I do except creep back upstairs,
Back to my room alone?'
You ask me in your letter which I read
In London next the newspaper outspread
With headlines 'Barcelona Fallen'
– Panic – street fighting – thousands fled –
Bringing this day each day my daily bread
The penny-dreadful fear that you are dead.

But still your stories go on running through my head.

For example, in Valencia, of the funeral
Of your uncle, the great general.
With downcast, sober eyes, you saw your aunt
Dressed black from head to foot, kneel down in front
Of the great coffin where her husband lay
In uniform, his medals on display.
Then, from your corner of the room, you saw
A troop of ants set out across the floor
And climb a table leg, to vanish in
The nearest corner of the coffin,
Passing diagonally right through it
Out at the corner opposite
And down that table leg, each with
A morsel of the general in its teeth.
And then you saw your aunt rise from her prayers
Leaving behind a small black pool, her drawers,
As final tribute to her husband's wars.

And then there was that aristocrat
Lost in the hills near Malaga
Having descended from his carriage
To follow for five days, on foot, a partridge.
Was it his brother who died broken-hearted,
At having failed to breed a green-eyed bull?

The stories go on running through my head . . .

It's not so much I hear the words you said
As that I see the laughter through the ruins . . .

I think that a circumference
Of flaming fragments forms a Catherine wheel,

At whose centre the unturning axle
Stays steady like an eye that gazes through
Our world exploding, just as you
Stand at your window looking at me

And seem to smile.

IV   A SEPARATION

Song

Stranger, you who hide my love
    In the curved cheek of a smile
And sleep with her upon a tongue
    Of soft lies that beguile,
      Your paradisal ecstasy
    Is justified is justified
By hunger of the beasts beneath
    The overhanging cloud
      Who to snatch quick pleasures run
      Before their momentary sun
Be eclipsed by death.

Lightly, lightly from my sleep
    She stole, our vows of dew to break
Upon a day of melting rain
    Another love to take:
      Her happy happy perfidy
    Was justified was justified
Since compulsive needs of sense
    Clamour to be satisfied
      And she was never one to miss
      Plausible happiness
Of a new experience.

I, who stand beneath a bitter
       Blasted tree, with the green life
Of summer joy cut from my side
       By that self-justifying knife,
          In my exiled misery
       Were justified were justified
If upon two lives I preyed
       Or punished with my suicide,
          Or murdered pity in my heart
          Or two other lives did part
To make the world pay what I paid.

Oh, but supposing that I climb
       Alone to a high room of clouds
Up a ladder of the time
And lie upon a bed alone
       And tear a feather from a wing
And listen to the world below
And write round my high paper walls
       Anything and everything
Which I know and do not know!

The Little Coat

The little coat embroidered with birds
Is irretrievably ruined.
We bought it in the spring.
She stood upon a chair
And raised her arms like branches.
I leaned my head against her breast
Listening to that heavy bird
Thudding at the centre of our happiness.

Everything is dragged away.
The clothes that were so gay
Lie in attics, like the dolls
With which wild children used to play.
The bed where the loved one lies
Is a river bed on which
Enchanting haunting life
Is carried where the current may –
Tangled among blocks of ice,
Nests and singing branches
Were the Springs of yesterday.

The Double Shame

You must live through the time when everything hurts
When the space of the ripe, loaded afternoon
Expands to a landscape of white heat frozen
And trees are weighed down with hearts of stone
And green stares back where you stare alone,
And the walking eyes throw flinty comments,
And the words which carry most knives are the blind
Phrases searching to be kind.

Solid and usual objects are ghosts
The furniture carries cargoes of memory,
The staircase has corners which remember
As fire glows redder in gusty embers
And each empty dress cuts out an image
In fur and evening and summer and spring,
Of her who was different in each.

Pull down the blind and lie on the bed
And clasp the hour in the glass of one room
Against your mouth like a crystal doom.
Take up the book and stare at the letters
Hieroglyphs on sand and as meaningless –
Here birds crossed once and a foot once trod
In a mist where sight and sound are blurred.

The story of others who made their mistakes
And of one whose happiness pierced like a star
Eludes and evades between sentences
And the letters change into eyes which read
The story life writes now in your head
As though the characters sought for some clue
To their being transcendently living and dead
In your history, worse than theirs, but true.

Set in the mind of their poet, they compare
Their tragic sublime with your tawdry despair
And they have fingers which accuse
You of the double way of shame:
At first you did not love enough
And afterwards you loved too much
And you lacked the confidence to choose
And you have only yourself to blame.

Elegy for Margaret

In memory of Margaret Spender, died Christmas Day, 1945

I

Darling of our hearts, drowning
In the thick night of ultimate sea
Which (indeed) surrounds us all, but where we
Are crammed islands of flesh, wide
With a few harvesting years, in our own lives disowning
The bitter salt severing tide;

Here in this room you are outside this room,
Here in this body your eyes drift away,
While the invisible vultures feed on
Your life, and those who read the doom
Of the ill-boding omens say
The name of a disease which, like a villain

Seizes on the pastures of your life
Then gives you back some pounds of flesh, only again
To twist you on that rack of pain
Where the skeleton shows through you like a knife,
The weak eyes flinching with still hoping light
That, where we wait, deceives our hoping sight

Until hope signs us to despair – what lives
Seems what most kills – what fights your fate
Loses most strength – and the loved face which smiles
Mirrors the mocking illness which contrives,
Moving away some miles
To ricochet again at the fixed date.

Least of our world, yet you are most our world
Here, where the well are those who hide
In dreams of life painted by dying desire
From violence of our time outside;
Where those who most live are most often hurled
With heroic eyes through waters shot with fire.

So, to be honest, I must wear your death
Next to my heart, where others wear their love,
Indeed it is my love, my link with life
My word of life being death upon my breath.
My dying word because of you can live
Crowned with your death, so not evading truth.

II

From a tree choked by ivy, rotted
By yellow spreading fungus on the bark
Out of a topmost branch
A spray of leaves is seen
Spreading against the sky its mark
As though the dying tree could launch
The drained life of the sap
Into one final shoot
Above the shining, lapping circling evergreen.

So with you, Margaret,
Where you are lying,
The strong tree of your limbs dragged back
By those cords that choke,
How difficult is dying
In your dying eyes.

How tediously the clock kills
When your fading breath
Launches one usual word
Through that stillness of death.
A trickling water fills
The sad well of your body
With gradual drops of dying
– Yet all the love we knew
Still lights upon your eyes.

Oh how, when you have died,
Shall we remember to forget
And with knives to separate
This death from this life –
Since, darling, there is never a night
But the restored pride of your youth
With all its flags does not float
Upon my sleep as on a boat.

III

Poor girl, inhabitant of a strange land
Where death stares through your gaze
As though the cold moon
Shone through midsummer days
With the skull-like glitter of night:

Poor child, you wear your summer dress
And your shoes striped with gold
As the earth wears a variegated cover
Of grass and flowers
Covering caverns of destruction over
Where hollow deaths are told.

I look into your sunken eyes
Shafts of wells to both our hearts
Which cannot take part in the lies
Of acting these gay parts.
Under our lips, our minds
Become one with the weeping
Of the mortality
Which through sleep is unsleeping.

Of what use is my weeping?
It does not carry a surgeon's knife
To cut out the wrongly multiplying cells
At the root of your life.
It can only prove
That extremes of love
Stretch beyond the flesh to bone
Howling in dark alone.

Oh, but my grief is thought, a dream,
Tomorrow's gale will sweep away.
It does not wake every day
To the facts which are and do not seem:
The granite facts around your bed,
Poverty-stricken hopeless ugliness
Of the fact that you will soon be dead.

IV

(i)

Already you are beginning to become
Fallen tree-trunk with sun-burnished limbs
In an infinite landscape among tribal bones
Encircled by encroaching ritualistic stones

(ii)

Those that begin to cease to be your eyes
Are flowers parched of their honey where memories
Crowd over and fly out like avid butterflies.
The striped and glittering colours of lost days,
Swallow-tail, Red Admiral, fritillaries,
Feed on your eyes and then fly from our gaze.

(iii)

In the corner of the bed you are already partly ghost
Whispering scratching existence almost lost
To our blatant life, which spreads through all the rooms
Our contrast, transient as heaped consoling blooms.

(iv)

You are so quiet; your hand on the sheet seems a mouse,
Yet when we look away, the flails
Which pound and beat you down with ceaseless pulse
Shake like a steam hammer through the house.

(v)

Evening brings the opening of the windows,
Now your last sunset throws
Shadows from trees,
Atrean hounds it unleashes
In front of a sky in which there burns a rose.
The Furies point and strain forwards
The pack of night is crowding towards us.

V

The final act of love
Is not of dear and dear
Bluebird-shell eye pink sea-shell ear
Dove twining voice with dove:

O no, it is the world-storm fruit
Sperm of tangling distress,
Mouth roaring in the wilderness,
Fingernail tearing at dry root.

The deprived fanatic lover,
Naked in the desert
Of all except his heart,
In his abandon must cover

With wild lips and torn hands,
With blanket made from his own hair,
With comfort made from his despair,
The sexless body in the sands.

He follows that bare path
Where the flesh guides to the skull
And the skull into hollows, full
Of delirium and death.

Dazed, he sees himself among
Saints, who slept with leprous sins,
Whose tongues grow on such ruins
And such a wild fire is his tongue –

'How far we travelled, sweetheart,
Since that day when first we chose
Each other as each other's rose,
And put all other worlds apart.

'Now we assume this coarseness
Of loved and loving bone
Where all are all and all alone
And to love means to bless
Everything and everyone'

VI

To H.S.

Dearest and nearest brother
No word can turn to day
The freezing night of silence
Where all your dawns delay
Watching flesh of your Margaret
Wither in sickness away.

Yet those we lose, we learn
With singleness to love.
Regret stronger than passion holds
Her these times remove:
All those past doubts of life, her death
One happiness does prove

Better in death to know
The happiness we lose
Than die in life in meaningless
Misery of those
Who lie beside chosen
Companions they never choose.

Orpheus, maker of music,
Clasped his pale bride
Upon that terrible river
Of ghosts of those who died.
Then of his poems, the uttermost
Laurel sprang from his side.

When your red eyes follow
Her body dazed and hurt
Under the torrid mirage
Of delirious desert
Her breasts break with white lilies,
Her eyes with Margaret.

Yet to accept the worst
Is finally to revive
When we are equal with the force
Of that with which we strive
And having almost lost, at last
Know that such was to live.

As she will live who, candle-lit,
Floats upon her final breath,
The ceiling of the frosty night
And her high room beneath,
Wearing not like destruction, but
Like a white dress, her death.

[96]

VI   AMBITION

The Public Son of a Public Man

Old man, with hair made of newspaper cutting
A public platform voice,
Tail coat and top hat strutting
Before your constituents' applause –

When a child, my dreams rode on your wishes,
I was your son, high on your horse,
My mind a top whipped by the lashes
Of your rhetoric, windy of course.

Before I could speak I had learned my lesson
Better never be born at all
Than live in this world and fail to impress on
Time, our name SPENDER in letters inch-tall.

Father, how we pitied those who had let
The emptiness of their unknown name
Fade on a rose and die in secret
Far from our trumpeting posthumous fame.

How shall we know that we really exist
Unless we hear, over and over,
Our egos through the world insist
With all the guns of the self-lover?

And when the weight of all time's darkness
Presses upon our shuttered fall
How shall we know, if our lives went markless,
That we have lived at all?

Father, imagine one day my sorrow
At school, when I watched the other boys' faces
Turn from your prize-giving speech – their tomorrow
Plastering your yesterday with their grimaces?

Then you lay in your grave, for the first time alone.
Devoured by worms, by newsprint forgotten,
Superseded, pelted down,
By our generation, still more rotten.

When I left your funeral, my face was hard
With my contempt for your failure still.
But, father, the hardness was a scabbard
For your resurrected will.

Through my tears there broke the fire
Of a prophetic son's anointment.
Seeking to spread your name like Empire,
It was then I made my appointment

With fame, beyond the gates of Death.
How like an engine now I press
Towards that terminus, last breath,
The Bitch Goddess called success.

Posterity will watch the spaces
Where, from an incorruptible mine,
Yours and my names take their places
Among the tinsel stars that shine.

But sometimes I stand as though beyond a wall
Outside a drunkard's face, where a child seems hidden,
And I remember being lost when I was small
In a wilderness, a garden.

If I had the key, I would return
There where the lovers lie, locked on bright grass,
Prisoners and the homeless make me yearn
With homesickness when I pass.

O father, to a grave of fame I faithfully follow
Yet I love the glance of failure, tilted up,
Like a gipsy's amber eyes that seem to swallow
Sunset from the evening like a cup.

The Furies

I

In the theatre
The actors play the rituals of their parts
– Captains, killers, lovers, clowns –
At the end falling on those swords
That open windows to the audience
Those who consider their lives different
From the enacted play of passions.
But which are actors, truly, which the audience –
The players who only simulate
Or the spectators dangling from their fate?
Where is the true performance
Finally sweeping actors and audience
Into a box, at curtain fall?

Believing, both of them, the real unreal,
They are stared down on by the universe
Staging in their lives its play of passions.

II

O brave powdered mask of motherhood
For twenty years denying that the real
Was ever anything but the exceptional,
You were an excellent stage-manager,
For your son's sake, your great house his theatre
Where all the plays were musicals, or light;
'This is the stage where nothing happens that can matter
Except that we look well produced and bright.'

Your problem was no easy one
Somehow to spare your only son
The gloomy brooding of his father's eyes,
After the war, for twenty years
Pacing the lawn between two wars,
His sombre way of staring at the table.
You were courageous and capable
Gaily you called these things his 'moods',
Just 'moods', 'moods', like anything else.
A chair, the empty clanging of alarm bells.

You rebuilt the Georgian house, returfed the lawn,
Planted the kitchen garden in its wall.
And the servants in the servants' hall,
Tidying the downstairs rooms at dawn.
You bought a fishing rod, a pony and a gun
And gave these serious playthings to your son.

The fresh air and the scenery did the rest.
He ripened and his laughter floated on the lake,
A foretaste of those memories that now suggest
His photograph with shirt open at the neck.
He came downstairs to dinner 'dressed'.
Then your triumphant happiness bound cords
Around his laughing glance like a blue bow.
Catching your husband's eye, your eyes spoke words
'This is the world. We've left the furies below.'

If a guest came, and in the course
Of gossip, spoke of 'so-and-so's divorce'
Or else 'Poor Lady X, she died of cancer',
You had your fine frank answer,
Questioning him with vivid curiosity
Poverty, adultery, disease, what strange monstrosity!
You smiled, perhaps, at your guest's eccentricity,
Dragging such specimens out on your floor.

Your son grew up, and thought it all quite real.
Hunting, the family, the business man's ideal,
The poor, and the unhappy had his sympathy,
They were the exceptions, born to prove his rule
And yet he had his moments of uneasiness
When, in the dazzling garden of his family,
With the green sunlight tilted on your dress,
His body suddenly seemed an indecency,
A changeling smuggled to the wrong address.

Still, he got married. *She* was dull of course.
But everything had turned out quite all right.
The bride sailed on the picture page in white.
She looked a little hard, in the hard light.
Your son wore uniform. You, now mother-in-law,
Who'd brought him up into a world at war,
At last felt tired. You wondered what he knew of life,
Whether enough to satisfy his wife.
Perhaps he'd learned from nature or his horse.

Oh, but in vain
Do men bar themselves behind their doors
Within the seemly and appointed house
Delineating life as they would see it,
By the fireside, in the garden, round the table.

The storm rises
The thunderbolt falls, and how feeble
Is the long ritual
Made sacred to respect by all appearance,
Though up-to-date its shell
Strengthened with steel and concrete.

The walls fall, tearing down
The mother-of-pearl inlaid interior.
The cultivated fire leaps from the grate
Consumes the house, the cat reverts to tiger
Leaping out of a world changed back to jungle
To claw her master.

The parents fall,
Clutching at beams that snap like straw.
The handsome only son
Tanned leader of his village team
Is shaken out of the silk folds
Of sprinkled lawns, as from a curtain.

He is thrown out on to a field abroad.
A whip of lead
Strikes a stain of blood from his pure forehead.
Into the dust he falls,
Oval face carved from a mother's kisses
Eternally chaste ivory
Staring up at the sun, the eyes at last wide open.

Tom's a-Cold

Such a day such a day when the rain
Makes earth and sky one dark plain

When noon is a mirror of mud
And the moon will be river of blood

Such a day such a day all my life
On this plain in this house with my wife.

I went clothed in herringbone tweed
A grey shell in which my bald head

Seemed a walnut, so wrinkled and lined.
The chips of blue eyes were my mind.

I sat through my life as at table
Pre-posthumously respectable.

Looking down at my plate I could see
Time's worms gnawing back at me.

Then I'd go for a ride on my bicycle
Down the country lanes, mile on mile,

And I'd think 'How everything descends
Black clouds trailing horse tail ends

And at fairs, country folk with their hopes
Like puppets dangled from ropes

By a god who will soon set them down
Six feet deep, with emperor and clown.'

Preachers said 'Life ascends, like a plant,'
But to me things seemed all aslant,

Diagonal pressure of rain
Waters driving down under the plain.

A tumulus outlined the strata
Where arrow-flints pointed to data

Of primal cities deep underground
Where hierarchic bones interwound

With shards, ever cruder in shape
Back to ancestral ape.

I loved old attics where the lumber
Of past centuries seemed to slumber:

Faded silks, hip baths, warming pans,
Rhinoceros horns, flint locks, pistols, sedans

Imagining ladies and gentlemen –
Muslin pokes, furs, cloaks, they were snug in.

Such musings made it incumbent
I sympathize with the recumbent

The drunkard in his ditch of facts,
The furthest gone in all their acts.

I noted the wish of prostitutes
To sleep prematurely among roots,

I observed the lad's or the great lady's mouth
Tormented with desire like drought.

Such I understood, I was there with all
Who break their lives against a wall

Or who in action or in thought
Out of their drab condition wrought

Some passionate purpose which would prove
Their deepest need their greatest love

I understood the sick botched lives,
The drink, the whoring and the knives.

Well, what I abhorred were the great claims
Of those with superhuman aims

The wars, the abstract cause, proud knowledge
Exalting imperial privilege

And in faith's name, the dubious creed
Usurping the single human need

Of knowing that we nothing know
Of where we came from, where we go

And nothing have, except we can
Comfort that poor condition, man.

They called me pessimist in my day
Yet perhaps I was happier than they,

Living in life as in the fallow
Earth which I now lie below.

Within life always, as in the bone,
Part of mankind and thus alone.

I lived within my hollow minute
Like the tune within the flute,

And where the tune breathed through the hole
You may call, if you like, my soul.

VII SPIRITUAL EXPLORATIONS

Spiritual Explorations

For Cecil Day Lewis

We fly through a night of stars
Whose remote frozen tongues speak
A language of mirrors, mineral Greek
Glittering across space, each to each –
O dream of Venus and Mars.
In a dome of extinct life, far far far from our wars.

I

Beneath our nakedness, we are naked still.
Within the mind, history and stars expose
Our bodies' frailty and a new day blows
Away huts and papyri of the will.
    The Universe, by inches, minutes, fills
Our tongues and eyes where name and image show
With words and pictures. Star and history know
Their legends in our minds, time kills.
    Revolving with the earth's rim through the night
We conscious fragments, pulsing blood and breath,
Each separate in the self, yet reunite
For that dark journey to no place or date
Where, naked beneath nakedness, beneath
Our human generation, we await
The multitudinous loneliness of death.

II

You were born, must die; were loved, must love;
Born naked, were clothed; yet naked walk
Under cloth flesh; ghosts move
Hollow, hollow, hollow, under clock-talk, star-talk.
    Time and space upon you feed;
Upon your eyes, their far horizons;
Upon your heart, their searing need;
Upon your death, empty significance.
    There is one fate beneath that ignorance,
All humanity, of which you are part,
O Self of flesh and thought and breath:
Chalk-faced, diamonded harlequin, it
Strums on your gut such songs and pleasant dances,
Amor, O solitude, O seldom death.

III

Since we are what we are, what shall we be
But what we are? We are, we have
Six feet and seventy years, to see
The light, and then release it for the grave.
    We are not worlds, no, nor infinity,
We have no claims on stone, except to prove
In the invention of the city
Our hearts, our intellect, our love.
    The tower we build soars like an arrow
From the earth's rim toward the sky's,
Upwards or downwards in a pond,
Climbing or diving from the self, to narrow
The gap between the world behind the eyes
And the receding universe beyond.

[114]

IV

That which divides, joins again in belief.
We see the inextricable knots that bind
Each in himself, thus seeing we are blind,
The eye the witness of our prisoned grief.
  Each rounded life gnaws at its little leaf
Of here and now; each bound within its kind;
Only world outside within the mind
Tempts with its prize each one to be a thief.
  People are not aeons, they are not space
Not empires, not maps; they have only
Bodies and graves. Yet all the past, the race,
Knowledge and memory remain unfurled
Within the individual, lonely
With time, winning, losing, his world.

V

The immortal spirit is that single ghost
Of all times past incarnate in each time
Which through the breathing skeleton must climb
To be within our living minds engrossed.
Without that spirit within, our selves are lost,
But shadows haunting the earth's rim.
Unless we will it live, that spirit dims,
Dies in our lives, its death, our death, the cost.
  One sacred past, present, futurity
Seeks within our many-headed wills
To carve in stone the dove, the flame-winged city.
Shut in himself, each blinded subject kills
His neighbour and himself, and shuts out pity
For that sole making spirit which fulfils.

VIII   WAR POEMS

In memory of
William Sansom,
writer and fireman

The War God
(The Fall of France, 1940)

Why cannot the one good
Benevolent feasible
Final dove, descend?

And the wheat be divided?
And the soldiers sent home?
And the barriers torn down?
And the enemies forgiven?
And with no retribution?

Because the conqueror
Is the instrument of power
That hammers his heart
Out of fear of former fear.
When those he now vanquishes
Vanquished his hero-father
Surrounding his cradle
With fabled anguishes.

Today his victory
Chokes back fierce anxiety
Lest children of these slain
Prove dragon teeth sown,
Now their sun goes down,
Sprout tomorrow again
Stain the sky with blood
And avenge their dead fathers.

The killed, filled with lead,
On the helpless field
May dream pious reasons
Of mercy, but alas
They did what they did
In their own high season.

The world is the world
And not the slain
Nor the slayer forgive.
There's no heaven above
Ends passionate histories
In unending love.

Yet under wild seas
Of chafing despair
Love's need does not cease.

Air Raid Across the Bay at Plymouth

I

Above the whispering sea
And waiting rocks of black coast,
Across the bay, the searchlight beams
Swing and swing back across the sky.

Their ends fuse in a cone of light
Held for a bright instant up
Until they break away again
Smashing that image like a cup.

II

Delicate aluminium girders
Project phantom aerial masts
Swaying crane and derrick
Above the sea's just surging deck.

III

Triangles, parallels, parallelograms,
Experiment with hypotheses
On the blackboard sky,
Seeking that X
Where the raider is met
Two beams cross
To chalk his loss.

IV

A buzz, felt as ragged but unseen
Is chased by two Excaliburs of light
A thud. An instant gleams
Gold sequins shaken from a black-silk screen.

V

Round the coast, the waves
Chuckle between rocks.
In the fields, the corn
Rustles with metallic clicks.

The Conscript

On the turf's edge – grass flashing like a knife –
The conscript stands above his native city.
He sees the sun's last rays before that night
Whose tunnelled dark will swallow up the life
He's known, to thrust him on the war tomorrow.
He gazes on a sky that shows no pity.
The sunset builds the furnace of his sorrow.

The violence of tomorrow seems so real,
Discipline that will take him so defined
This evening is the buried life he feels
Turned yesterday already in his mind.
The sun, now sunk, belonged to a gold past
The happiness of childhood left behind
More shining by tomorrow's bitter contrast.

But now, beyond the rising star, appear
The armies marching to an earlier war.
The skeleton who strides last strikes a drum
The conscript's soul is summoned to his eyes.
'Father,' he cries, 'Father, Behold, I come!'

Rejoice in the Abyss

The great pulsation passed. Glass lay around me
Resurrected from the end. I walked
Along streets of slate-jabbering houses,

Against an acrid cloud of dust, I saw
The houses kneel, revealed each in its abject
Prayer, my prayer as well: 'Oh God,
Spare me the lot that is my neighbour's.'

Then, in the upper sky, indifferent to our
Sulphurous nether hell, I saw
The dead of the bombed graveyard, a calm tide
Under the foam of stars above the town.

And on the roof-tops there stood London prophets
Saints of Covent Garden, Parliament Hill Fields,
Hampstead, Hyde Park Corner, Saint John's Wood,
Crying aloud in cockney fanatic voices:
'In the midst of Life is Death!' They kneeled
And prayed against the misery manufactured
In mines and ships and mills, against
The greed of merchants, vanity of priests.
They sang: 'We souls from the abyss
To whom the stars are fields of flowers,
Tell you: Rejoice in the abyss!
For hollow is the skull, the vacuum
In the gold ball, St Paul's gold cross.
Unless you will accept the emptiness
Within the bells of foxgloves and cathedrals,

Each life must feed upon the deaths of others,
The shamelessly entreating prayer
Of every house will be that it is spared
Calamity that strikes its neighbour.'

A Man-Made World

What a wild room
We enter, when the gloom
Of windowless night
Shuts us from the light

In a black malicious box.
A freezing key locks
Us into utter dark
Where the nerves hark

For the man-made toys
To begin their noise.
The siren wails. After,
Broomsticks climb the air,

Then clocks burst their springs,
Then the fire-bell rings.
Above and below comes
Thunder of the drums.

Oh, what white rays gleaming
Against the sky's crouched ceiling!
What sudden flashes show
A face that cries 'Oh!'

In darkness where we are,
With no saving star,
We hear the world we made
Pay back what we paid:

Money, steel, fire, stones,
Stripping flesh from bones,
With a wagging tongue of fear
Tormenting the ear,

Knocking at the outer skin,
To ask if any soul is in,
While the gloom descends
On our means become our ends.

Epilogue to a Human Drama

When pavements were blown up, exposing wires,
And the gas mains burned blue and gold,
And brick and stucco were pulverized – a cloud
Pungent with smells of mice, corpses, anxiety.
When the reverberant emptied façades
Of West End theatres, shops and churches,
Isolated in a vacuum of silence, suddenly
Cracked and blazed and fell with the seven-maned
Lions of Wrath, licking the stony fragments –

Then the sole voice heard through deserted streets
Was the Cassandra bell which rang, released
To quench those fires that ran through city walls.
London burned with unsentimental dignity,
Of resigned kingship. Banks and palaces
Stood near the throne of domed St Pauls
Like courtiers round the royal sainted martyr.
August shadows of night
And flares of concentrated light
Dropped from the sky to paint a final scene
Illuminated agony of bursting stone.

Who can wonder then that every word
In burning London, stepped out of a play?
On the stage there were heroes, maidens, fools,
Victims, a Chorus. The heroes won medals,
The fools spat quips into the skull of death,
The wounded waited with the humble patience
Of animals trapped within a cellar
For the pickaxes to break with light and water.
The Chorus assisted, bringing cups of tea.

IX   HOME

For Natasha, Matthew and Lizzie

The Dream

'You dream', he said, 'because of the child
Asleep in the nest of your body, who dreams.'

He smiled.

He put his head weighed with a thought
Against her lips. Thus locked

They felt the life their lives had wrought
Moving within her flesh: complete
Between their cradling bodies rocked.
The future folded crowing street.

One

Here then
She lies
Her hair a scroll along
Her neck the grooved warm nape
Her lips half-meeting on a smile
Breath almost unbreathing
A word this word my love upon the white
Linen
As though I wrote her name out on this page.

Here we
Are one
Here where my dreaming wakes upon her sleep
One within one

And a third hidden meeting in the child.

Absence

No one is perfection, yet
When, being without you, I console
Myself, by dwelling on some blemish
Once marked, which now might mar the whole,
Telling myself your absence might become my wish,

Oh then, that blemish which I set
Between us, vanishes.
I see only the pure you in your eyes,
Remembering how they light
With mine. All that between us lies
Is opened like a gate
Through which our memories unite
The oneness of their wishes.

Absence has the quality of ice
On a high peak, above a landscape of snow:
It is a lens which magnifies
The valley of the roofs below.
Blank light shines
On the home faces, surrounding them with white
As though flesh were the halo of the eyes.

Arrows of light pierce through the mist,
Lapis lazuli has pressed
Its burning way through smothering clouds
To show upon the world your face which seems
A miracle among macabre dreams,
Like a madonna painted on a shroud.

The Trance

Sometimes, apart in sleep, by chance,
You fall out of my arms alone,
Into the chaos of your separate trance.
My eyes gaze through your forehead, through the bone,
And see where, in your sleep, distress has torn
Its violent path, which on your lips is shown
And on your hands and in your dream forlorn.

Restless you turn to me, and press
Those timid words against my ear
Which thunder at my heart like stones.
'Mercy!' you plead. Then 'who can bless?'
You ask. 'I am pursued by Time,' you moan.
I watch that precipice of fear
You tread, naked in naked distress.

To that deep care we are committed
Beneath the wildness of our flesh
And shuddering horror of our dream,
Where unmasked agony is permitted.
Our bodies stripped of clothes that seem,
And our souls, stripped of beauty's mesh,
Meet their true selves, their charms outwitted.

This pure trance is the oracle
That speaks no language but the heart,
Our angel with our devil meets
In the atrocious dark nor do they part
But each each forgives and greets,
And their mutual terrors heal
Within our love's deep miracle.

Empty House

To M.F.M.S.

Then, when the child was gone
I was alone
In the house suddenly grown vast. Each noise
Explained its origin –
Animal, vegetable, mineral,
Nail, creaking board, or mouse.
But mostly there was quiet of after battle
Around the room where lay
The soldiers and the paint-box, all the toys.
    Then, when I went to tidy these away
My hands refused to serve:
My body is the house,
Each plaything that he touched, a nerve.

To My Daughter

Bright clasp of her whole hand around my finger
My daughter, as we walk together now.
All my life I'll feel a ring invisibly
Circle this bone with shining: when she is grown
Far from today as her eyes are far already.

Nocturne

Their six-weeks-old daughter lies
In her cot, crying out the night. Their hearts
Are sprung like armies, waiting
To cross the gap to where her loneliness
Lies infinite between them. This child's cry
Sends rays of a star's pain through endless dark;
And the sole purpose of their loving
Is to disprove her demonstration
Of all love's aidlessness. Words unspoken
Out of her mouth unsaying, prove unhappiness
Pure as innocence, virgin of tragedy,
Unknowing reason. Star on star of pain
Surround her cry to make a constellation
Where human tears of victims are the same
As griefs of the unconscious animals.

Listening, the parents know this primal cry
Out of the gates of life, hollows such emptiness,
It proves that all men's aims should be, all times,
To fill the gap of pain with consolation
Poured from the mountain-sided adult lives
Whose minds like peaks attain to heights of snow:
The snow should melt to wash away such grief
Unceasing love should lave the feet of victims.

Yet, when they lift their heads out of such truths
Today mocks at their prayers. To think this even
Suffices to remind them of far worse
Man-made, man-destroying ills which threaten
While they try to lull a child. For she
Who cries for milk, for rocking, and a shawl,
Is also subject to the rage of causes
Dividing nations. Even at this moment
Eyes might fly between them and the moon
And a hand touch a lever to let fall
That which would make the street of begging roofs
Pulverize and creep skywards in a tower:
Down would fall baby, cradle and them all.

That which sent out the pilot to destroy them
Was the same will as that with which they send
An enemy to kill their enemy. Even in this love
Running in shoals on each side of her cot
Is fear, and hate. If they shift their glances
From her who weeps, their eyes meet other eyes
Willing death, also theirs. All would destroy
New-born, innocent streets. Necessity,
With abstract head and iron feet, men's god
Unseeing the poor amulets of flesh
Unhearing the minutiae of prayer.

Parents like mountains, strongholds of their child,
Envallied here beneath them, also hold
Upon their frozen heights, the will that sends
Destruction into centres of the cities
Which concentrated locked centennial peace
For human generations to indwell.

Hearing their daughter's cry which is the speech
Of indistinguishable human life
They know the dark is filled with means which are
Men's plots to murder children. They know too
No cause is just unless it guards the innocent
As sacred trust: no truth but that
Which reckons this child's tears an argument.

Boy, Cat, Canary

Our whistling son called his canary Hector.
'Why?' I asked. 'Because I had always about me
More of Hector with his glittering helmet than
Achilles with his triple-thewed shield.' He let Hector
Out of his cage, fly up to the ceiling, perch on his chair, hop
On to his table where the sword lay bright among books
While he sat in his yellow jersey, doing his homework.
Once, hearing a shout, I entered his room, saw what carnage:
The Siamese cat had worked his tigerish scene;
Hector lay on the floor of his door-open cage
Wings still fluttering, flattened against the sand.
Parallel, horizontal, on the rug, the boy lay
Mouth biting against it, fists hammering boards.
'Tomorrow let him forget.' I prayed, 'Let him not see
What I see in this room of miniature Iliad –
The golden whistling howled down by the dark.'

X   LANDSCAPE AND SEASCAPE

In Attica

Again, again, I see this form repeated:
The bare shadow of a rock outlined
Against the sky; declining gently to
An elbow: then the scooped descent
From the elbow to the wrist of a hand that rests
On the plain.
                    Again, again,
That arm outstretched from the high shoulder
And leaning on the land.
                              As though the torsoed
Gods, with heads and lower limbs broken off
Plunged in the sky, or buried under earth,
Had yet left arms extended here as pointers
Between the sun and plain:
                              had made this landscape
Human, like Greek steles, where the dying
Are changed to stone on a gesture of curved air
Lingering in their infinite departure.

Seascape

In Memoriam M.A.S.

There are some days the happy ocean lies
Like an unfingered harp, below the land.
Afternoon gilds all the silent wires
Into a burning music for the eyes.
On mirrors flashing between fine-strung fires
The shore, heaped up with roses, horses, spires
Wanders on water tall above ribbed sand.

The motionlessness of the hot sky tires
And a sigh, like a woman's from inland,
Brushes the instrument with shadowy hand
Drawing across those wires some gull's sharp cry
Or bell, or shout, from distant, hedged-in, shires;
These, deep as anchors, the hushing wave buries.

Then from the shore, two zig-zag butterflies
Like errant dog-roses cross the bright strand
Spiralling over waves in dizzy gyres
Until they fall in wet reflected skies.
They drown. Fishermen understand
Such wings sunk in such ritual sacrifice

Remembering legends of undersea, drowned cities.
What voyagers, oh what heroes, flamed like pyres,
With helmets plumed, have set forth from some island
And them the seas engulfed. Their eyes
Distorted to the cruel waves' desires
Glitter with coins through the tide scarcely scanned,
While, far above, that harp assumes their sighs.

Lost Days

For John Lehmann

Chalk Blue

The Chalk Blue (clinging to
A harebell stem, its loop,
From which there hangs the flower
Shaken by the wind that shakes
The butterfly also) –
Opens now, now shuts, its wings,
Opening, closing, like a hinge,
Sprung at touch of sun or shadow.
    Open, the wings mirror
All the cloudless sky.
Shut, the milky underwing
Cloud-mirroring, is bordered by
Orange spots nailed there
By a pigmy hammering.

Drowned under Grass

Then, when an hour was twenty hours, he lay
Drowned under grass. And watched the carrier ant
With mandibles as trolley, push in front
Wax-yellow specks across the parched, cracked clay.

A tall sun made the stems down here transparent.
Moving, he saw the speedwell's sky-blue eye
Start up below his own, a chink of sky
Fallen on the floor of his grass tent.

He pressed his mouth against the rooted ground
Held in his arms, he felt the earth spin round.

Mosquito in Florence

Florentine mosquito
Afloat on black air
Anchors above my head,
Tinsel trumpet blowing
In the tomb of my ear.
Angel of Fra Angelico
Awakening me, dead,
To such thoughts as make
Midnight Judgement Day.

The Barn

Half hidden by trees, the sheer roof of the barn
Is a river of tiles, warped
By winding currents of weather
Suns and storms ago.

Through beech leaves, its vermilion shows
A Red Admiral's wing, with veins
Of lichen and rust, an underwing
Of winter-reft leaves.

Now, in the spring, a sapling's jet
Gold-green, cuts across
The low lead gutter. Leaves hold up
Red tiles reflected in their cup.

   At the side of the road where cars crash past,
The barn lies under the sky – a throat
Full of dark gurgitation:

A ghost of a noise, a hint of a gust,
The creak of a winch, the wood of a wheel
Caught in the rafters centuries ago.

   Entangled in murmurs, as in a girl's hair,
Is the enthusiastic scent
Of straw – gold in that sunbeam
Which, laden with motes, strikes across the floor.

Dusk

Steel edge of plough
Thrusts through the stiff
Ruffled fields of turfy
Cloud in the sky.
Above charcoal hedges
And dead leaf land
Cuts out a deep
Gleaming furrow
Of clear glass looking
Up a stair of stars.

On earth below
The knotted hands
Lay down their tasks,
And the wooden handles
Of steel implements
Gently touch the ground.
The shifting animals
Wrinkle their muzzles
At the passing peace,
Like bells, of the breeze;
And the will of Man
Floats loose, released.

The dropping day
Encloses the universe
In a wider mantle
Than meridian blaze.
A terracotta blanket
Of dark, robs one by one
Recognition from villages,
Features from flowers,
News from men,
Stones from the sun.

All the names fade away,
With a spasm, nakedness
Assumes mankind.
Men's minds cast adrift
On beds in upper rooms,
Awaiting the anchorage
Of sleep, see more
Than a landscape of words.

The great lost river
Crepitates
Through creeks of their brains.
Long-buried days
Rise in their dreams.
Their tight fists unclose
The powers they hold,
The manners and gold.

Then the burning eye
Of a timeless Being
Stares through their limbs
Drawing up through their bones
Mists of the past
Filled with chattering apes,
Bronze and stone gifts,
From all continents
Of the tree of Man
The sun of this night
Mocks their dark day
Filled with brief aims
– Stealing from their kind
Killing their kind
They turn with a groan
From terror of love
Back to their daybreak of
Habitual hatred.

Remembering Cincinnatti, 1953

For John Betjeman

Remember how
Twenty-five years ago in Cincinnati
At the end of winter,

          May
Fountained with blossom the first new sky
– Japanese double cherry peach plum – petals
White pink and mauve cupped in gold leaf.

But that same night
Driven from Arctic down the plains
A blizzard whirled through dark with knives of ice
And scarves of snow.

          Yet when
We woke next morning that dervish had passed on.

The innocuous sun
Imperturbably re-entered
The clean-swept dome of sky become
A deeper wept-out blue.
          Each leaf and blossom
– Japanese double cherry peach plum – petals
White pink and mauve cupped in gold leaf,
Was separately enclosed in ice.

They glittered in their millions in the sun.

Within an hour the ice had melted, petals dropped
Like moulted pigeon feathers slush on sidewalks
Trampled by galoshes
Of shoppers passing on their errands.

XI DIARY POEMS

Driving Through Snow

Driving along the road and looking
Through cleaned glass where screen-wipers weave
Twin circumferences, I see
Shadows and lights among which wheels
Make time on space. My brain
Is drugged by the inpouring emptiness
Through which I stare between the trees
That line the road each side, with branches
Like feathers shaking feathers. To keep awake,
I must persuade myself this fairy stage
Is solid, and not swansdown. If
I crossed those margins or met head-on
Those white owl headlights flying towards me
I'd be the killer or the killed. I have to
Fix my mind on friends, the firelit
End to this journey: or else on
The work that must not end before begun.

(Connecticut, 1971)

Grandparents

We looked at Matthew's child, our granddaughter,
Through the glass screen where eight babies
Blazed like red candles on a table.
Her crumpled face and hands were like
Chrysalis and ferns unrolling.
'Is our baby a genius?' he asked a nun.
We went to the Uffizi and he looked at
Italian primitives, and found
All their *bambini* ugly.
He started drawing Maro and her daughter
Nine hours after Saskia had been born.

(Florence, 1971)

Auden at Milwaukee

Dined with Auden. He'd been at Milwaukee
Three days, talking to the students.
'They loved me. They were entranced.'
His face lit up the scene.
I saw there the picture of him, crammed into
Carpet bag clothes and carpet slippers
His face alone alive alone above them.
He must have negotiated himself into the room
Like an object, a prize, a gift that knows his worth,
Measuring his value out to them on scales,
Word weighed by word, absorbed in his own voice.
He knows they're young and, better, that he's old.
He shares his distance from them like a joke.
They love him for it. This, because they feel
That he belongs to none, yet gives to all.
They see him as an object, artefact, that time
Has ploughed criss-cross with all these lines
Yet has a core within that purely burns.

(28 February 1970, New York)

[159]

Art Student

With ginger hair dragged over
                              fiery orange face,
Blue shirt, red scarf knotted round his neck
Blue jeans, soft leather Russian boots
Tied round with bands he ties and unties when
His feet are not spread sprawling on two tables –
Yawning, he reads his effort. It's about
A crazy Icarus always falling into
A labyrinth.
                 He says
He only has one subject – death – he don't know why –
And saying so leans back scratching his head
Like a Dickensian coachman.
                       Apologizes
For his bad verse – he's no poet – an art student –
– Paints – sculpts – has to complete a work at once
Or loses faith in it.
                  Anyway, he thinks
Art's finished.
                There's only one thing left –
Go to the slaughter house and fetch
A bleeding something-or-other – oxtail, heart,
Bollocks, or best a bullock's pair of lungs,
And put them in the college exhibition,
On a table or hung up on a wall
Or, if they won't allow that, just outside
In the courtyard.
                   (Someone suggests
He put them in a plastic bag. He sneers at that.)

The point is, they'll produce some slight sensation –
Shock, indignation, admiration. He bets
Some student will stand looking at them
For hours on end and find them beautiful
Just as he finds any light outside a gallery,
On a junk heap of automobiles, for instance,
More beautiful than sunsets framed inside.
That's all we can do now. Send people back
To the real thing
                        – the stinking corpse

                                            (Connecticut, 1970)

From My Diary

'She was', my father said (in an aside),
'A great beauty, forty years ago.'
Out of my crude childhood, I stared at
Our tottering hostess, tremulous
In her armchair, pouring tea from silver –
Her grey silk dress, her violet gaze.
I only saw her being seventy,
I could not see the girl my father saw.

Now that I'm older than my father then was
I go with lifelong friends to the same parties
Which we have gone to always.
We seem the same age always
Although the parties sometimes change to funerals
That sometimes used to change to christenings.

Faces we've once loved
Fit into their seven ages as Russian dolls
Into one another. My memory
Penetrates through successive layers
Back to the face which first I saw. So when the last
Exterior image is laid under its lid,
Your face first seen will shine through all.

XII WORD

Word

The word bites like a fish.
Shall I throw it back, free
Arrowing to that sea
Where thoughts lash tail and fin?
Or shall I pull it in
To rhyme upon a dish?

A Question of Identity

Who he was, remained an open question
He asked himself, looking at the Others –
The Strangers, roaring down the street.

Explorer, politician, bemedalled
General, professor, any of these
He might have been, but he was none.

Impossible, though, to avoid the conclusion
That he had certain attributes: for instance,
Parents, birthdays, sex. Calendars

Each year the same day accused him of his age,
Also, he was a husband and had children,
And fitted to the measure of his desk,

Yet he never felt quite certain
Even of certainties: discerned a gap
(like that between two letters) between statistics,

Those he was always writing out on forms,
And his real self. Sometimes he wondered
Whether he had ever been born, or had died . . .

Was a space yearning for some asterisks . . .
*   *   *   *   *   *
*   *   *   *   *   *

Sometimes he had the sensation
Of being in a library, and reading a history

And coming to a chapter left unwritten
That blazed with nothing . . . nothing except him
. . . Nothing but his great name and his great deeds.

The Generous Days

His are the generous days that balance
Spirit and body. Should he hear the trumpet
Echoing through skies of ice –
And lightning through his marrow –
At once one with that cause, he'd throw
Himself across some far, sad parapet,
Spirit fly upwards from the sacrifice,
Body immolated in the summons.

But these too are the days when, should he greet
Her who goes walking, searching for a brooch
Under plantains at dusk beside the path,
And sidelong looks at him as though she thought
His glance might hide the gleam she sought –
He would run up to her and each
Find the lost clasp hid in them both,
Mindless of spirit, so their bodies meet.

Body spirit, spirit body, breath
Or death, the shadow of his will –
In these, the generous days, to prove
His utmost being simply is to give –
Wholly to die, or wholly, else, to live.
If the cause ask for death then let it kill.
If the love ask for blood then let it move.
Giving is all to life or all to death.

After, of course, will come a day not this
When he'll be taken, stripped, strapped to a wheel
Which is a world and has the power to change
The brooch's gold, the trumpet's golden blaze,
The lightning through the blood those generous days,
Into what drives a system, like a fuel.
Then to himself he will seem loathed and strange
Have thoughts yet colder than the thing he is.

Sleepless

Awake alone in the house
I heard a voice
– ambiguous –
With nothing nice.

Perhaps knocking windows?
A board loose in the floor?
A gap where a draught blows
Under the door?

Repairs needed? Bills?
Is it owls hooting – pay! –
Or it might be the walls
Crumbling away.

Reminding – 'you, too,
Disintegrate
With the plaster – but you
At a faster rate'.

Or it might be that friend once
I shut outside
Sink or swim – well, he sank –
In my sleep cried

'Let me in! Let me in!'
Tapping at the pane.
Him I imagine.
Twenty years in the rain.

Awaking

Ever the same, forever new!
The gravel path searching the Way;
The cobwebs beaded with the dew;
The empty waiting of new day.

So I remember each new morning
From childhood, when pebbles amaze.
Outside my window, the forewarning
Glitter of those days.

The sense felt behind darkened walls,
Of an amber-solid world, a lake
Of light, through which light falls,
It is this to which I wake.

Then the sun shifts the trees around
And overtops the sky, and throws
House, horse and rider to the ground
With knockout shadows.

The whole sky opens to an O,
The cobweb dries, the petals spread,
The clocks grow beards, the people go
Walking over their graves, the dead.

The world's a circle where all moves
Before after, after before.
Such joy my fresh-awaking proves
Each day – until I start to care.

Subject, Object, Sentence

A subject thought: because he had a verb
With several objects, that he ruled a sentence.
Had not the Grammar willed him these substantives
Which he came into as his just inheritance?

His objects were *wine*, *women*, *fame* and *wealth*.
And a subordinate clause – *all life can give*.
He grew so fond of having these that, finally,
He found himself becoming quite subjective.

Subject, the dictionary warned means 'Someone ruled by
Person or thing'. Was he not *having*'s slave?
To achieve detachment, he must be *objective*
Which meant to free himself from the verb *have*.

Seeking detachment, he studied the context
Around his sentence, to place it in perspective:
Paraphrased, made a critical analysis,
And then re-read it, feeling more *objective*.

Then, with a shock he realized that *sentence*
Like *subject–object* is treacherously double.
A sentence is condemned to stay as stated –
As in *life-sentence*, *death-sentence*, for example.

XIII REMEMBERING

One More New Botched Beginning

Their voices heard, I stumble suddenly, remembering
Ten years ago, here in Geneva
I walked with Merleau-Ponty by the lake.
Upon his face, I saw his intellect.
Energy of the sun-interweaving
Waves, electric, danced on him. His eyes
Smiled with their gay logic through
Black coins flung down from leaves.
                                        He who
Was Merleau-Ponty that day is no more
Irrevocable than the I that day who was
Beside him – I'm still living!

  Also that summer
My son stayed up the valley in the mountains.
One day I went to see him and he stood
Not seeing me, watching some hens.
Doing so, he was absorbed
In their wire-netted world. He danced
On one leg. Leaning forward, he became
A bird-boy. I am there
Still seeing him. To him
That moment – unselfknowing even then
Is drowned in his oblivious early days.
                                        Such pasts
Are not diminished distances, perspective
Vanishing points, but doors
Burst open suddenly by gusts
That seek to blow the heart out . . .

                              Today, I see
Three undergraduates standing talking in
A college quad. They show each other poems –
Louis MacNeice, Bernard Spencer and I.
Louis caught cold in the rain, Bernard fell
From a train door.

Their lives are now those poems that were
Pointers to the poems they made their lives.
We read there in the college quad. Each poem
Is still a new beginning. If
They had been finished though they would have died
Before they died. Being alive,
Is when each moment's a new start, with past
And future shuffled between fingers
For a new game . . .
                              I'm dealing out
My hand to them, one more new botched beginning
There, where we still stand talking in the quad.

Louis MacNeice

Like skyscrapers with high windows staring down from

                                                the sun,

Some faces suggest
Elevation. Their way-up eyes
Look down at you diagonally and their aloof
Hooded glance suggests
A laugh turning somersaults in some high penthouse
Of their skulls. Seeing such a one
Looking down at you, smiling to himself, you can't help
Looking down at yourself from his point of view: at the

                                                top of

Your bald head, for instance
Where the one brushed-back copper-dyed hair is noted
With precise irony. Louis
MacNeice was
Like that. Leaning
Against a marble chimney piece
With one elbow an angle in a Picasso cubist portrait,
The superior head slanted back
With dancing eyes summing you up
And laughter only just arrested
At some joke about you, known only to himself
(Perhaps the cutting phrase sharpening in his forehead)
He half-beckoned you up into his high mind
For a shared view of your clumsiness –
I mean, me, of mine.

Now, reading his poem 'Bagpipe Music', I don't know how

                                                to pronounce

C-e-i-l-i-d-h – nor what it means –
He looks down from high heaven
The mocking eyes search-lighting
My ignorance again.

Ice

(Vienna)

For Muriel

She came in from the snowing air
Where icicle-hung architecture
Strung white fleece round the Baroque square.
I saw her face freeze in her fur
From the chimney corner of the room
Where I had waited in my chair.
I ran to her with my lips' fire
I kissed that warmth against her skin
And felt the red make the white bloom
When, at my care, her smiling eyes
Shone with the brilliance of the ice
Outside, whose dazzling they'd brought in.
   That day, until this, I forgot.
How is it now I so remember
Who, when she came indoors, saw not
The passion of her white December?

A Girl Who Has
Drowned Herself Speaks

If only they hadn't shown that cruel mercy
Of dredging my drowned body from the river
That locked me in its peace, up to their surface
Of autopsy, and burial and forms –
This, which was my last wish, might have come true –
That when the waves had finally washed away
The remnants of my flesh, the skull would stay –
But change to crystal. Things outside
Which it had looked at once, would swim into
Eye sockets that looked at them: through
The scooped-out caverns of the skull, would dart
Solid phosphorescent fish, where there had been
Their simulacra only in the brain.

Cyril Connolly

This makes of you your statue.
Chisels away the flesh
Lays bare the intellect,
The brow pure semi-circle
Star-striking dome.

Ferlum sidera vertico.

Deep in the mouth's crevasse
The silent tongue savours
Only the must of dying.

Finally, the head is Roman.

Late Stravinsky Listening to Late Beethoven

'At the end, he listened only to
Beethoven's last quartets.
Some we played so often
You could only hear the needle in the groove.'

She smiled,
Lightly touching her cheek.

I see you on your bed under the ceiling
Weightless as your spirit, happiness
Shining through pain. You have become
Purged of every self but the transparent
Intelligence, through which the sounds revolve
Their furious machine. With delectation
You watch Beethoven rage, hammer
Crash plucked strings, escape
On wings transfiguring horizons: transcend
The discords in his head that were
The prisoning bars of deafness.

                              He only knew
That there was music which went on outside
That in his mind, through seeing sound: for example,
Walking through the Wiener Wald
One loud spring day, he saw a shepherd
Playing his flute against the hillside,
And knew there was the tune because he saw it
Delineated by the flute.
Then stumping down the fields into the valley,
Saw cymbals clash beneath steep banks
Where, on the river, blocks of ice
Collided: saw too, high up,
The wind pluck strings of willow harps
Against the brass of sky.
                              His eyes became
Windows in the skull through which he looked
Out on a world of sound.
                              Above
A base of mountain peaks, a bird, a violin,
Sustains a curve, a tune, parabola,
Held in the eye become an ear: flies on
Until the line at last dissolves
Into that light where the perceiver
Becomes one with the thing perceived,
The hearing with the seeing,
                              Beethoven
Released from deafness into vision,
Stravinsky in that music from his dying.

Auden's Funeral

I

One among friends who stood above your grave
I cast a clod of earth from those heaped there
Down on the great brass-handled coffin lid.
It rattled on the oak like a door knocker
And at that sound I saw your face beneath
Wedged in an oblong shadow under ground.
Flesh creased, eyes shut, jaw jutting
And on the mouth a grin: triumph of one
Who has escaped from life-long colleagues roaring
For him to join their throng. He's still half with us
Conniving slyly, yet he knows he's gone
Into that cellar where they'll never find him,
Happy to be alone, his last work done,
Word freed from world, into a different wood.

II

But we, with feet on grass, feeling the wind
Whip blood up in our cheeks, walk back along
The hillside road we earlier climbed today
Following the hearse and tinkling village band.
The white October sun circles Kirchstetten
With colours of chrysanthemums in gardens,
And bronze and golden under wiry boughs,
A few last apples gleam like jewels.
Back in the village inn, we sit on benches
For the last toast to you, the honoured ghost
Whose absence now becomes incarnate in us.
Tasting the meats, we imitate your voice
Speaking in flat benign objective tones
The night before you died. In the packed hall
You are your words. Your listeners see
Written on your face the poems they hear
Like letters carved in a tree's bark
The sight and sound of solitudes endured.
And looking down on them, you see
Your image echoed in their eyes
Enchanted by your language to be theirs.
And then, your last word said, halloing hands
Hold up above their heads your farewell bow.
Then many stomp the platform, entreating
Each for his horde, your still warm signing hand.
But you have hidden away in your hotel
And locked the door and lain down on the bed
And fallen from their praise, dead on the floor.

III

(Ghost of a ghost, of you when young, you waken
In me my ghost when young, us both at Oxford.
You, the tow-haired undergraduate
With jaunty liftings of the head.
Angular forward stride, cross-questioning glance,
A Buster Keaton-faced pale *gravitas*.
Saying aloud your poems whose letters bit
Ink-deep into my fingers when I set
Them up upon my five-pound printing press:

'An evening like a coloured photograph

A music stultified across the water

The heel upon the finishing blade of grass.')

IV

Back to your room still growing memories –
Handwriting, bottles half-drunk, and us – drunk –
Chester, in prayers, still prayed for your 'dear C.',
Hunched as Rigoletto, spluttering
Ecstatic sobs, already slanted
Down towards you, his ten-months-hence
Grave in Athens – remembers
Opera, your camped-on heaven, odourless
Resurrection of your bodies singing
Passionate duets whose chords resolve
Your rows in harmonies. Remembers
Some tragi-jesting wish of yours and puts
'Siegfried's Funeral March' on the machine.
Wagner who drives out every thought but tears –
Down-crashing drums and cymbals cataclysmic
End-of-world brass exalt on drunken waves
The poet's corpse borne on a bier beyond
The foundering finalities, his world,
To that Valhalla where the imaginings
Of the dead makers are their lives.
The dreamer sleeps forever with the dreamed.

V

Then night. Outside your porch we linger
Murmuring farewells, thinking tomorrows
Separate like those stars above.
Gone from our feast, your life enters your poems
Like music heard transformed into notes seen.
Your funeral dwindles to its photograph
In black and white, of friends around your grave.
This dark obliterates all. Farewell,
The magic instrument of consciousness
With intellect like rays exposing
Lives driven out on the circumference
Of this time, their explosion: O, but making
Paradigms of love, the poems
That draw them back into the circle,
Of your enfolding solitude.

XIV CHORUSES FROM
The Oedipus Trilogy

From *Oedipus Rex*

O thrilling voice of Zeus
           come from Apollo's golden shrine
           with what intent towards us

                I tremble I faint I fail
                terror racks my soul

O Delian healer to whom my cries
from this abyss of despair arise

                What fate unknown until now
                or lost in the past and renewed
drawn from the revolving years
                will you send to us

O speak o tell me, immortal voice

                To Athena, daughter of Zeus,
           and her sister, Artemis,
                and Apollo of fiery arrows
           triple guardians of Thebes
                           I call

If ever before in time past
you saved us from plague or defeat
                turn back to us now, and save

The plague invades
No knowledge saves
birth pangs of women
bring forth dead their children
life on life sped
to the land of the dead
like birds wing on wing
struck down from their flying
to the parched earth
by the marksman death

O Delian healer hear my prayer
star of my hope in my night of despair

grant that this god who without clash of sword on shield
fills with cries of our dying Thebes he makes his battlefield
    turn back in flight from us
        be made to yield

    driven by great gales favouring our side

to the far Thracian waters wave on wave
where none found haven ever but his grave

    O Zeus come with thy lightning to us
                      save

    And come back Bacchus
hair gold-bound and cheeks flame-red
    whom the Bacchantae worship and the Maenads led
    by his bright torch on high

Revelling again among us Bacchus and make death
The god whom gods and men most hate lie dead.

[192]

II

If I still have the gift of prophecy,
O hills and valleys of lovely Cythaeron,
I swear that by tomorrow at full moon
Oedipus will recognize in you
Mother and nurse and native land he grew in.
So these, because they pleased our king, we sing
And to Apollo may they too prove pleasing.

Who was it fathered you, and who conceived you,
Child, among these hills, by moon or noon?
Was it to Pan some wandering nymph bore you
While he roamed the mountainside? Or may it have been
Some bride Apollo favoured? Or even
Bacchus, god of the Bacchantae, received you,
A gift from a nymph on Helicon,
One of those he most delights to play with?

III

O human generations, I consider
Life but a shadow. Where is the man
Ever attained more than the semblance
Of happiness but it quickly vanished?
Oedipus, I count your life the example
Proving we can call no human blessed.

With skill incomparable he threw the spear;
He gained the prize of an unchallenged fame;
He killed the crooked-taloned maiden
Whose singing made the midday darken;
He was our tower that rose up against death
And from that day we called him King of Thebes.

[193]

But now whose history is more grievous
Plagued with the loss of all that greatness his?
Whose fortune ever met with such reverse?
I pity Oedipus for whom that soft flesh couch
That bore him, also proved his nuptial couch,
Oh how can soil in which your father sowed
Have secretly endured your seed so long?

Time, all-revealing, finally tracked you down,
Condemned the monstrous marriage which begot
Your children upon her, your own begetter.
O son of Laius, would my eyes had never seen you.
I weep like one with lips formed for lament.
Until today it was you who gave me light;
Today your darkness covers up my eyes.

From *Oedipus at Colonos*

Stranger, this is shining Colonos,
Famed for horses, loveliest place.
Nightingales pour forth their song
From wine-dark depths of ivy where they dwell
Close to the god's inviolable bowers,
Heavy with fruit and never visited
By scorching sun or rending wind.
Here Dionysus revelling runs
The nymphs that nursed him, his companions.

Each dawn narcissus clusters, washed
In the sky dew, upraise their crowns,
Those worn of old by the great goddesses,
And crocuses like shafts of sunlight show.
Fed by eternal streams, the fountains
Of Cephysus fan through the plains
Bringing their swelling breasts increase.
Nor are the Muses absent from this place.

And here a miracle, a thing unknown
In Asia, flourishes perpetually –
The self-renewing vast-trunked olive tree,
A bastion for us against enemies
And, for Athenian children, nurturer.
Nor youth nor age can cause it damage
For Zeus smiles on it, and grey-eyed
Athena holds it in her keeping gaze.

But most of all, I have to praise the horse,
Poseidon's gift to this land, glorious,
Running beside white horses of the waves.
And Colonos is where Poseidon taught
Man bit and bridle for the horse the horse
To tame the wild colt and to curb his speed:
And taught him carve the wood for prows and oars
Chasing the Nereids through the waves.

II

Whoever craves a longer life than his allotted span
That man
I count a fool. For what do more days add
But to his sum of grief, and not of pleasure,
If he endure beyond the appointed measure?

The curtain falls the same, in any case.
When his superfluous days are done;
Youth, wedding, dance, song, death itself
Are one.

Best, never to have been born at all; the next best is
Quick turn back to nothing whence he came.

For after tasting youth's soon-passed
Feather-head follies, then what troubles
Do not crowd in on him:
Faction, envy, murder, wars, and last
Senility claims its own:
Unsociable,
Infirm, unfriended, shunned by all.

Oedipus is old: a promontory
Exposed on every side to storms
The elemental forces overwhelm,
Every disaster falling on him: come
From sunrise and the sunset, from
The icy north, torrid meridian,
All day – and all night long, the glittering stars.

From *Antigone*

Happy are those who never tasted evil.
For once the house incurs the rage of heaven
The indignant curse fallen on it never ceases
But remains always, and for ever passes
From life to life through all its generations.

So from the earliest times the sorrows
Of children of the house of Labdacus
Heap on their dead new sorrows always
Never set free by later generations,
And if a son arise to free that house
A god arises soon to cast him down.

Just as when howling gales from off-shore
Pile up in mountainous waves the Thracian seas
Fathoms above the shadowy sea floor,
These suck up from the depths black sands
Which, risen, spread over all the surface
While the storm roars against the headlands.

Now, of the house of Oedipus, that hope
Which was the last extension of the root,
That light which promised so much is put out,
By bloodstained dust that was a debt
Unpaid to the infernal gods,
And by a young girl's frenzied heart.

Index of Titles and First Lines

[199]

[201]

[203]